best new poets
2006

Eric Pankey, Editor

Jeb Livingood, Series Editor

Copyright © 2006 by Jeb Livingood

This book was published by Samovar Press, Charlottesville, Virginia,
in cooperation with *Meridian,* www.readmeridian.org. For additional information
on *Best New Poets,* see our Web site at www.bestnewpoets.org.

Cover photograph by Uwe Nölke

Text set in Adobe Garamond Pro

Printed by Thomson-Shore, Dexter, Michigan

ISBN 13: 978-0-9766296-1-0
ISBN 10: 0-9766296-1-5
ISSN 1554-7019

In memory of Jim Simmerman
—E.P.

In memory of Sally Stuart
—J.L.

Contents

Introduction

Welcome to *Best New Poets 2006*, our second installment of fifty poems from emerging writers. In these pages, the term "emerging writer" has a narrow definition: here, it means someone who has yet to publish a book-length collection of poetry. Like the rules for many anthologies, that one is, perhaps, arbitrary. But the main goal of *Best New Poets* is to provide special encouragement and recognition to new poets, the many writing programs they attend, and the magazines that publish their work. And, of course, to deliver an accessible, eclectic sampling of emerging poets to you, the reader.

From April to June of 2006, *Best New Poets* accepted nominations from each of the above sources. For a small reading fee, writers could upload two poems to a Web site, www.bestnewpoets.org, as part of our Open Competition. A month earlier, writing programs from around the United States and Canada had sent nominations of up to two writers, whom *Best New Poets* later solicited for work. And the anthology also asked literary magazines across North America to send two of their best recent poems by writers who met our definition of "emerging." We asked that the poems submitted either be unpublished or published after June 15, 2005. So, not only do new writers appear in this anthology, you're also seeing some of their latest work.

In all, we received submissions from nearly 1,200 poets, with some 2,000 poems uploaded to our system—nearly double the number in 2005. A pool of four dedicated readers blindly ranked the submissions, and 175 finalists went on to this year's editor, Eric Pankey, for his final winnowing to fifty. Like last year's edition, we were especially pleased that so many of the final selections came from the Open Competition. Two of those Open Competition poets, Teresa Ballard and Vincent Zompa, also received cash prizes for their outstanding work.

There are many people I need to thank, the most important being the four readers I briefly mentioned above, Lilah Hegnauer, Jennifer Chang, Aaron Baker, and Terence Huber. All of them are practicing poets, and the care they took with the manuscripts, the thoughtfulness of their comments, was inspiring. Thanks as well to Sharmila Voorakka, whose input on several early submissions proved invaluable, and especially to Kevin McFadden and Angie Hogan, two readers from 2005, whose editorial advice helped shape this year's edition. Of course, I must also thank Eric Pankey, this year's editor, who had the toughest reading job of all—and was correspondingly paid the least. His efforts set the editorial bar very high, and in 2007, I'm not sure where I can find a guest editor with Eric's enthusiasm and affinity for young writers.

I should also thank Jason Coleman and Mark Saunders for their efforts to have *Best New Poets 2006* marketed and distributed by the University of Virginia Press. It is a relief to have some real pros take over.

Even so, I think you could argue that the final print anthology is less important than the process that creates it. By process, I'm not talking about typesetting or editing, but instead, the process that begins when literary magazines re-read their recent issues to decide which two poems are among their very best from emerging writers. The process that begins when writing programs ask participants to send in work. The process that begins when hundreds of poets select some of their own writing, save two poems in a word processing file, and send a few million electrons hurtling through cyberspace. The process that begins when poets read *Best New Poets 2006* and see works from *Sentence, AGNI, 32 Poems,* or *FIELD,* and think, *There's a publication that's willing to take a chance....* The process that begins when one emerging poet reads another emerging poet's work—and is humbled.

In a world that does not always value the solitude and introspection it takes to make poems like these, it is somehow reassuring that such a process goes on at all. And judging by these poems—and the many fine submissions that did not make this year's final selections—there is a quiet minority out there, working steadily, every day.

—*Jeb Livingood*
University of Virginia

best new poets
2006

Teresa Ballard

I Am Thinking of My First Deer

A doe, her legs spread open
in the back of my father's truck,
her body a brown map near blue sky.
My father turns her over, she is the color of earth.
She's warm and my fingers smell of sage
and blood. I piece her together in my mind
as my brothers remove her skin.
I give her back her body, the same way
I was promised Jesus would return to us on earth.
I am thinking of my first deer
because you are sleeping
and underneath your lids, your eyes are open.
My fingers smell slightly of things broken
and I realize you are always afraid
of the way I open myself,
how I must swallow up every sadness.
I wonder if somehow I've always known you.
If you have returned in another form
leaving behind the fur of your death.

—Open Competition Prize Winner

Stephanie Lenox

Making Love to Leopard Man

> Tom Leppard…has approximately 99.9%
> of his body covered in tattoos…
> a leopard-skin design.…[He] now lives
> as a hermit on the Isle of Skye.
> —*Guinness World Records*

Though I'm not a needle, let me touch you.
Let me look into the pink secret of your ear.
Let me part, one by one, your reclusive, unmarked toes.

Trust me, you are not the first man I've known
who thought he was an animal, who's sharpened
his claws without knowing what to do with them.

Like continents your bruise-green spots drift apart.
Lying beside you, I watch the ink bleed slowly
into the tiny channels of skin, edges blurring

into your yellow sea. One-hundred-six islands
I've counted so far: that one looks like a storm cloud,
that one at your hip like the head of a woman.

You're not the only one who knows how to make
the body an elaborate disguise. How I wish
the children who torment you would throw stones

at the ugly hut of my life and scatter like birds
when I glare at them. I want to bathe my scars
in the isle's dirty river. I want fangs.

Let me show you how hermit crabs do it: tap
my borrowed shell until I uncurl like a raw finger,
exposing myself to salt. Out there, I could be eaten,

I could be carried by the current into the mouth
of prey. Hold me closer with your human claws.
For now, let's pretend we have nothing to hide.

—Nominated by the University of Idaho

Kiki Petrosino

You Have Made a Career of Not Listening

God has spider skin and lives in secret trees. I have stood beside you, saying this, as you reach into the cupboard for another stack of dry noodles. You eat them with the dead still on, with the sticky deadness still on, because you always throw out the foil package of seasoning. So the noodle brick just loosens, slowly, in a flat brine of city water, just squats and spreads in the center of the frying pan like a washed-up boxer or a stranger's face disappearing into morphine. After the fight the boxer wraps a towel around his hips and walks into his manager's office. Some boys wipe fifty bucks' worth of sweat from the ring, then head to the all-night diner smelling like stacks of thumbs. Meanwhile, dollar bills are blooming in the stranger's lonely raincoat pocket. It is 5:00 A.M. There are places you will never go with me, no matter how many times you ask, or how hard you eat.

—*Open Competition Winner*

Vincent Zompa

13 Stories

He had been a doctor in this village since anyone could remember
      patients with vapors   children like fawns

      She had been here before and it wasn't right the last time either
          the whirling and shining   smell of leaves

His name was Thunder of Moose, the son of the chief
    names in a cold ashtray   cigarettes dead

      She was a woman who talked incessantly, to stare down the Silence
        open mouth closed mouth   and the lunging

He was a pawn in a larger game and it was getting late
        each turgid player   buried in junk drawers

She was the type of woman who caved at every request
        the silken mouthed moth   alone in lamplight

He was the type of man who grew old right after high school
        God makes you kneel   you unpiece the self

Her white shirtsleeve reflected the moonlight as it flooded the porch
        waiting for crickets   sweatsuit couples pass

His eyes were always squinting and somewhere off in the distance
        her hair once fallow   the fortunate loam

She made love like a stone they sharpened knives with
        a treehouse with boys   a garage an old man

He made love like a drunk on a mechanical bull
        magazine lust   naming the stars

He was an entrepreneur yet loved music from the forest's edge
        the crush of his father   ceilings of green luster

It had become harder to breathe since the children
        his legs gone to dusk   her blue eyes the snow

—*Open Competition Prize Winner*

Gretchen Primack

Colors

I   Fuchsia

Bloated, unwieldy,
fat velvet

fibers to rub a cheek
then grind a smoke out in.

A Colette heroine
on heroin. Unspellable.

Plump lampshades.
My heart

when you cock
your head at me.

II   Chartreuse

A squint. A pint of over-frozen.
Contracted glands. A squirt.

Nineteen eighty five: Esprit,
Forenza, Ciao, Mia,

Samantha's dollar polish.
Silk wound around a redhead's

white waist. We're drunk on it,
you, me, and the redhead.

III   Puce

Four letters bound together
with straw, the color of wound,

sets of consonant-vowel quitting in pain
after two.

The color of the thought
of teeth against your teeth. I chewed

on that word until I *had* to stop—
Whose gift to language was this?

IV   Ecru

Everything has been washed out of me.
I'm coarse and the ground is coarser.

What is left? No berries, but plenty
of tough wide crisp

stalks. Circle here, aliens! Take the field!
The jaw goes slack. Lips dry

among the stalks. Nothing left
to talk about.

—Nominated by FIELD

Deborah Ager

The Problem with Describing Men

after Robert Hass

If I said lacerated light
In an unusually warm November.
If I said ice-cold palm on my inner thigh
And the way a tree opens its branches
When sun finally heats the garden.
If I said the power of a '67 Charger
Mixed with a detective's mystery.
If I said love, sometimes, yes, love
And jumping-from-a-moving-car anger.
Said the whir of a sander, the scent
Of birch, and tablespoons of sawdust.
What if I said night or a wave
Rocking into shore? If I said their names
One by one to the red sky? Said empty armchair?
Luck, dusky words, fight, torn photo.
What if I said moon? What if I said
White light dividing a lake in two?

—*Open Competition Winner*

Michael McGriff

Iron

I was wrong about oblivion then,
summer mornings we walked the logging roads
north of Laverne, the gypo trucks leaving miles of gravel dust
eddying around us. You were the *Queen of Iron*
and I, the servant *Barcelona.* The slash-pile
we tunneled through was the *Whale's Mouth,*
our kingdom. Jake-brakes sounded the death-cries
of approaching armies as they screamed over the ridge
where we held our little breaths and each other,
passing the spell of invisibility between us.
Five years later, you brought your father's
hunting knife to school and stabbed Danielle Carson
in the hip and I never saw you again.
I could say I left town for both of us, that I drove I-5 South
until I reached the aqueducts of California,
and for the first time felt illuminated before the sight
of water as it rushed beneath the massive turbines
spinning on the beige and dusty hills, powering a distant city
that would set me free. I could say
after your father covered the plastic bladder
of his waterbed with baby oil and wrestled you to it,

that in those days after your pregnancy I made plans
to drive a claw hammer into his skull. But I never left,
and when I moved it was only as far as the county line.
If my life has been a series of inadequacies, at least I know
by these great whirls of dust how beauty
and oblivion never ask permission of anyone.
In the book I read before bed, God lowers himself
through the dark and funnels his blueprints into the ear
of a woman who asked for nothing. Tomorrow night
she'll lead armies, in a few more she'll burn at the stake
and silver birds will rise from her mouth. This is the book
of the universe, where iron is the last element
of a star's collapse and the moon retreats each moment
into oblivion. My blood fills with so much iron I'm pulled
to a place in the hard earth where the wind
grinds over the ridge bearing the wheels of tanker trucks
oiling the access roads, where deer ruin the last of the plums,
where the sloughs shrink back to their deepest channels,
and I can turn away from nothing.

—*Nominated by* Northwest Review

Ciaran Berry

Topography with Storm Petrels & Arctic Tern

On our first television set, a black & white,
    the screen a square about the size of a trivet,
        my brother and I watch Van Gelderen sketch
an arctic tern. First, the circle of the head,

    its thick outline pointing towards the spiked
        prong of the beak, which, all in one stroke, gives
to the sleek curves of a throat that veers
    sharply towards the taut belly, then rises,

        splits into the twin prongs of the tail.
And then the back, then the wings opening.
    All of this happens at near double-speed,
        the fingers furious in their markings after

the charcoal's brief hover above the page.
    And now, his flits and feints having
        shaded out the only eye that's visible,
the glut of dark feathers around the crown,

some sleight of hand, or trick of editing,
        transmogrifies this stationary male into
a bird at wing above the outcroppings
    and crags of *Inis Mór*. Holding its own

        against the catch and drag of air, it looks
just like those two gray-brown storm petrels
    in Audubon's watercolor—one of fifty
        on display this week uptown. Already,

I've spent most of two afternoons wondering
    if they're rival lovers or a mating pair,
        one facing me, the other turned away,
their eyes fixed on each other in a gaze

    that can only mean hatred or ardor.
        And what they seem to say, strung up just so,
hanging forever between heaves of gale,
    is something about balance, about grace

        faced with the great weight of the elements.
According to Edward Armstrong, we know
    that during daylight birds use the sun to find
        their way, and that at night they rely on the stars.

It's thought that they may orient themselves
    using the earth's gravity, but there are aspects
        of how birds navigate that remain obscure.
Enough then to admire whatever drives

the wings, that heart no bigger than the tip
             of your middle finger, whatever name there is
for the desire that keeps the tern facing
             forward as it glides between hemispheres,

                  north to south and south to north again.
On his stalled crossing from Portsmouth,
             Audubon could not paint those storm petrels
                  as they hovered just above a cursive wave.

Instead, he spent those wild days below deck
             heaving the contents of his fraught stomach
                  into a laundry pail, trying hard to forget
it could be weeks before Liberty stuck her

             arm out of the fog, the *Colombia* bobbing
                  like a pink buoy, its jolts and jars dousing
the flame in his paraffin lamp, stirring
             whatever winged subject he carried home—

                  a tree pipit perhaps, or a chaffinch—to fix
its claws around the cage's bars and hold.
             In a Carna we will soon leave behind, so
                  that something small and feathered in us dies,

it is the year my brother and I find a jackdaw
             with a broken wing, the year the fish farm
                  where our father works closes its doors. The tanks
in the hatchery are emptied of oysters,

the mussel rafts are dragged ashore, and most
        of what we know vanishes like the wallet
and keys the magician picks from our old man's
        pockets as he assists with a trick at the circus,

        choosing a card, checking a bowler hat for holes.
Although all we know will never be returned.
        Lying on his bunk, nothing left to empty
        from his belly, Audubon stares through

an iced porthole at the almost black that runs
        beyond the eye and thinks of how his life
        will be a journey from one fixed point to another
with only open water in between, something

        he ought to take no pleasure in, yet the knowledge
        of it makes him almost happy. The chaffinch
is dying behind the bars and, in the morning,
        will be tossed overboard without even a word.

        And though Audubon will recover from this,
his latest bout of "the blue devils," he'll continue
        to suffer the erosions of the body until he can
        no longer lift a finger to enter the musculature

of a bird, until he can't even remember his own name.
        And I'm sure he'd know exactly what I mean
        when I explain that the future is a crew
of five or seven men in gray-brown overalls

who come to wrap the clocks and pictures
in blankets, to bear the couch and rocking chairs
out of that living room in which I sit
with my brother, eyes fixed on the screen,

hand hovering above a packet of crisps
as Van Gelderen's tern flies further and further
away, wings and body at first discernable,
then just a black dot, and then nothing.

—*Nominated by* The Missouri Review

Peter Kline

The Fire Meadow

A first snow fell on the fire meadow, where we stood.
Through ashen-skirted birches, the black brow of a gable.
Through birches, down the valley, just beyond the lake
that so soon would be coined and frozen, the heart-tree
shuddered: husks of blood and paper, a clatter of sticks.
We couldn't hear it. I remember there was no wind.
The snowflakes drew in measured lines against the earth's
magnet, scumbling the penciled margins of the tick-grass.

That was the day, or may have been the day, you said
I am not leaving you just as you left. The room
withdrew, as if the city at last had taken light
and burned completely, a black cloud against the sun.
Or might the room have been this meadow; the pale houses
birches; flames the ruff of snow chill at your throat?

—*Open Competition Winner*

Jennifer Chapis

The Beekeeper's Departure

I want to say there was an animal sound,
but even I know that's not true.

You simply rose into the sky
like a bone-made moon.

By the time I arrived, there remained
no coast to speak of.

Even the bees   silent.

History is not behind us.
I have trained myself to know

the open palm of your tongue—
supple like a plum in a breath-blue bowl.

In the end, all that matters is the shape of longing,
the eyes never quite whole enough.

A harem of bees brews like a promise.

(Think honey-bitterness, drying drop of sap.)
Burning logs *kack,*

shift in a fire pit, grief's weight
settling for gravity's sake.

I've known you better than anyone.
Two aged trees on a beach.

Horizon, blister about us.

—*Open Competition Winner*

Autumn Watts

Dry Lake, Nevada, 1983

MORNING
Ice in the rim of the water barrel. Sky so thin, the mountains rip holes in it. The dry lake in shadow; the mountains tipped white.

BOMBS
When they set off bombs underground I feel the ground hitch.

NEIGHBORS
A couple acres away there's a trailer with no door. A woman and five kids live in it. They block the door with plywood at night. Sometimes I hear a cat crying on the other side.

SATURDAYS
Me and Nina used to pick a direction and walk out that way straight into the lake. Once we found an old mattress, a bucket, beer cans. The mattress was bleached by the sun, with imprints.

FOUND
Another time we found a snake skull, followed by six vertebrae. The skull weighed nothing.

TEETH

When my horse died we had to tractor a hole, then push her into it. Her legs stuck up. My stepdad jumped in the hole, folded her legs to her belly. Her mouth hung open, and I saw her teeth. They were yellow, with brown stains near the top.

WIND

The wind blows all the time.

NIGHT

I can't see shit outside. The dark has texture: grains, phantom lights. Sky so thin the stars rip holes through it. I know the lake is out there, empty and silent.

WIND

Dust storms are white.

TEETH

My mom lost another one. They break off at the gumline. She takes horse penicillin for the infection. I ask her if it hurts. She says, "Yep."

FOUND

I startled a coyote from her nest. A moment frozen: her narrow snout, the bright, brief eye.

SATURDAYS

Some kids drove their truck into the lake last night. They were drunk, they thought the road continued but it was only the moon, shining off clay flats. The lake is dry. They didn't swim; they flew.

—Nominated by AGNI

Jessica Goodfellow

What You See If You Use Water as a Mirror

In Shinto, the eight elements
of beauty include impermanence
and perishability. Choose one
as your watermark. No,
that is the wrong one.

Begin by learning the 10,000 ways
to spell water. Puddle, swamp,
ice field: waters that don't
move. Estuary, geyser,
glacier: waters that do.

At lunch today, someone said
you were beautiful. The reader
is beautiful, he said. You weren't
there, but somewhere thinking
lagoon, waterfall, tide pool.

Knowing understatement is an element
of beauty, you thought drizzle,
fog, dew. All there is

to know about beauty can be learned
from water, so when you ask

the other five elements, you are told
mystery, incompleteness. Pause.
To learn the final three is to dishonor
the previous two. You must choose.
But here's a clue: cove, tributary, sleet.

—*Nominated by* Beloit Poetry Journal

Joe Wilkins

How to Bring Down Rain

First, listen to the old men, watch
their dry lips flap. Throw sheep

bones in the river, ribs and unlinked
wings of spine. See the water wet them.

It's possible. Shoulder the sun
and walk the fence line west. Wipe

an oily head of sweat on your t-shirt.
Now come in for lunch—tomato

sandwich, ice water, the easy chair
in the cellar where you open all

your father's books, breathe their inky
dust. Then dream him an old man,

dream him dead again, years later,
when fathers should die. Chase your

sister with a broken mouse, tell your
brother lies about the neighbor girl.

Though there's no water anymore,
crack off the ram's skull, toss it

in the river too. See the gravel smooth
as skin, and your mother's face—

like gravel. Look at her. Know God
does not hate you, that nine years

of drought is child's play. Now come
back to the old men, see them rise

from wooden chairs, hear their bones
sift the dust of yesterday's rain.

—*Open Competition Winner*

Andrew Allport

An Unknown Shore:
  Variations on a Fragment by Oppen

Cortez arrives.
      he is absolutely lost
at an unknown shore.
      and he is enraptured

(this is the nature of poetry

 The poem:

        Cortez arrives at an unknown shore
        he is absolutely lost
        and he is enraptured

Cortez arrives at an unknown shore
      he is utterly lost
      but he is enraptured

Cortez arrives too late.
      the shore is absolutely barren, the men lost
      to starvation and rapture

Cortez utters:
  "lost."

 (this is the nature of description

Cortez walks upon the beach.
  the ocean is as still as a map
  spread out on a table.

 (he takes a nap.

Cortez arrives, sun-senseless (?
  wrapped in gold
  ~~plashing in the shallow~~

  All the Cortezs arrive.
  all the waves arrive

 (this is the nature of disaster

     —Nominated by ZYZZYVA

Philip Pardi

Wintering

> *And as I walk the drifts of mingled sleet and snow,*
> *I pity these leaves and branches forced apart.*
> —Hsieh Hui-Lien

02.13.05.

Wind-kicked & ragged.
Mid-February.
Sun low like a lone headlight.

In search of winter, you find
wintering. Counters (of days),
hoarders (of seeds), collaborators

(in search of, in prayer for). In
air thick with cold
you find all warmth is local.

02.17.05.

Slippage & mule-time.
Umbrage of blankets.
A coarse cold, stars

pressed firmly in place.
Deer, perhaps a dozen, leap
the guardrail, one

by one
stepping through snow
as if through broken glass.

02.18.05.

You used to know.
Now, you used
to know. Small raft from *yes*

to *maybe,* little to show
for the long trek,
little to say but *rocks,*

watch for the rocks! Beyond hope
but this side of prayer
what's near is less near.

02.19.05.

Stepping outside, yesterday's prints
useless, a chill
between you & each thing

& you're arrayed against it,
each belabored step
a study in how long: socks

dry, fingers adroit. How winter
is a slowing for which
slowing is our best response.

02.21.05.

One month to the equinox.
Daylight earlier, sun higher
sooner, tho still at best a sideways

shine. No thing taller
than its shadow, a clear light
cast on winter's debris.

Eerie, the calm of *after*.
Nothing here but the bare limbs
of here.

02.24.05.

The speed of what will catch you
is constant
& tho you do your best

you too will grow slow
not unlike the cardinals
all winter at the feeder

till the young couple goes south
& they wait
& wait.

02.25.05.

How night brings everything
within reach.
The cedar you can't see

south of the house
may as well be pressed
against the window

& who's to say, from this chair,
you couldn't touch the woodshed?
For whom, right now, wouldn't you pray?

02.26.05.

Bird & bird flight, gone,
or so it seems to the speedy.
But then, walking outside long enough

to slow down enough
to look up & aside: wrens
in bare branches, the

thrill of chickadees
in spruces. Woodpeckers,
when they flee, flee far.

02.27.05.

Your way is warmth.
Your way is through
snow to the shed

& back, over & over
till the path hardens
into a line that will last into May.

Twice-gloved hands on an axe
with a nicked neck   everything
you do is about separation.

02.28.05.

Then, again, the odd bird-quiet calm of snow.
Hemlock & spruce skirts pinned.
The world recast

in whites & lines.
Stepping outside, nowhere to go
without leaving tracks.

The wait is the long haul—
a cursive cold,
standing still, stomping your feet.

03.01.05.

Small wonder, bowing,
tho later you ask: do we bend
or are we bent, is

the hinge above
or within?
Kneeling is small (you've seen

horses do it) but *wanting*
to kneel
startles.

03.04.05.

Five white inches
tho the earth, where wet,
remains dark, stream

& marsh taking it in
in stride. Dawn
above a generous snow

is no slow thing. Across
the road: the right-left-left-right
prints of a fox on the run.

03.05.05.

A neighbor, maple-
tapping, says
raccoon

but you cling to fox.
No sign of cardinals
for months

& you say
they didn't make it.
Always one truth over another.

03.09.05.

Thaw. Lay thee down but gently.
On their way back
to warmth, the feet burn.

On their way back to earth
leaves warm their way
through snow.

The earth
where before it cracked
now sags.

03.11.05.

Bird-bustle.
The sky unbruising itself.
What comes might not come

from a distance, could be
it was near
all along, an un-

furling.
I'm here—
the purest prayer.

03.14.05.

How in the forest, snow
falls twice, each
branch a cupped hand

that, come warmth,
uncups.
Each step

a step to the side
till you *were* here,
were waiting.

03.17.05.

Ice-melt & limb-fall,
a littering. Late winter's here
with its pocketful

of bookmarks, snow grown
wise to the ways of letting go.
What you take in

takes you on your way,
makes of debris a place to begin.
Squirrels emerge, walking atop.

03.18.05.

You look up
as far as the gutter
with its cargo of twigs

but even that slight leaning back
pulls the ladder away
& so you press close

forehead to hands
& the ladder returns
to the gable wall, *tap-tap,*

*

but when, moments later, you hear overhead
geese
you look up again

only higher   & the ladder
eases away again
its feet sinking deeper and deeper into what,

now,
is mud,
the ladder pausing, paused, upright—

—*Nominated by* Mid-American Review

Barbara Yien

Response to an Academic Question

The West: a place or a process?

Once I was a schoolgirl and the center of my compass was shoreline and fog. I was not concerned with my place in the world. The hands of my wristwatch told time and nothing more. If you had asked me the difference between suburb and city I'd have shown you the ocean. My parents were travel agents. I grew up and flew coach. I had something to say but my mouth was stuffed with fortune cookies. They were manufactured in Houston. One of them read: Enjoy nature, visit a park. Another one read: A good way to live longer is to eat more Chinese food. For a time I plowed rice fields in Hokkaido. That's a lie, I never made it to Hokkaido, but I came close. Li Po fell off his boat, Pound played telephone, and voila, modern poetry. Soon the easterners were dressing like the westerners who were showing up at cocktail parties decked in qi paos. *And the green grass grew all around all around, the green grass grew all around.*

—Open Competition Winner

Darren Morris

History's Sovereign

> *I, with no rights in this matter*
> —T. Roethke, Elegy for Jane

Maybe it is inescapable. Maybe it is alive and twisting like a hurricane up the coastline
      leaving only the frozen ash of a long beach, a cigarette cold in dawn's tray.
They are before rain and after, two thieves strung out on patience, drunk on
      a one-sided love affair with a brain-dead baby, who will soon die.

The father is choosing a suit today in which he will bury the child.
      He returns home with two: one black, one blue. The clerk told him
the suit makes the man, and the father sincerely hoped it would.
      For there was nothing left of himself, save paper and wind.

The mother has also stolen something that will kill her, and she knows it.
      At night she floats herself out with the child, holding him close to her
listening to his breath, listening for his voice, and imagined their raft
      going under the wave's wing. She can't help herself. She wants

to see where he goes—where he goes when he goes away.

I want to fold them all into this poem, they and their troubles. And I want to take
        the page it is written upon and place it in the large dresser drawer I no longer use
and I want to bury the dresser behind the farmhouse where I once stayed
        along with the dead horses and a junked piano's harp, too heavy to move.

So that someday the scientists will discover it and wonder, *What happened here?*
        The little prayer we whisper for the quick release of the child
expedites our own disappearance. And for everything that departs, something
        enters. Like this horseshoe from Millay's back pastures, deep fried in rust.

On it, two tacks hang like broken teeth, like a dead man buried in his dentures.
        At each tip of the shoe, two bulbous heads stood the heel of a dappled mare,
ridden least, for she was the most beloved. But to think of that small horse
        is to think of the violent upward curve, the bent half of the iron,

is to consider both its sudden fall and wonderment.

This is her shoe and the single wire, a bone-yellow piano key
        dislocated, a ligament searching the ghosted muscle of purest sound.
The wire is wrapped tight around the tips of its omega and nailed above the door,
        to let it empty like some lyre, until a note for what is missing

filled the highs of heaven with the moans of his lament.

When Percy Shelley drowned, his body was found washed ashore on the Italian coast.
        Two dragoons guarded him three days with their sad horses. Fearing cholera,
they coated him in lye and buried him inches deep, marking him with a flag.
        Then they drank wine and waited for Lord Byron and Mary to arrive.

When they did, they were ordered to burn him on a pyre. The strange thing was
　　　Shelley's body refused the fire. Then, suddenly, it burst like a match
as if his frozen veins were filled with fuel. His chest opened like a pod
　　　and there sat his heart, perfectly untouched, a golden apple.

Bryon could not help it. He walked up the ramp and stole it from the flame.

For the rest of her life the heart stayed with Mary, just as the blue lips of the child
　　　now stay with the mother, as the suits wait like crows on the hanger in the
closet. Byron dove in the sea and swam until he nearly drowned and when
　　　he got back on his feet, he was only rags and wind, and Shelley became

the bloom, whose petals nipp'd before they blew.

Yet the heart did not vanish when Mary died. It became something else, a sea wind
　　　churning an American storm that caused the men, pitching a game of shoes,
to run for cover back to the house, where Millay handed drinks each to each.
　　　The shoes were left in that field, the last one clanging off the spike

rolling out into *the uncut hair of the dead.*

Where it has returned to sew silent grief above our doors. Unlucky
　　　my house to lose an infant brother, unlucky theirs to be losing a baby,
to have no god whom god abandons, to have no choice
　　　all ye who enter here, to live as nothing but paper and wind.

And sing the last breath stolen from the blue lips of the child.
　　　Nothing will know that we are gone.

—*Open Competition Winner*

Alison Powell

Edema

My father says, *They might have to cut it off her.* Simple, like bone
and bone, her finger has fused with that old ring. She sits there,

mindless as plank wood, cawing in a starched hospice bed.
They'll use a tiny saw to do it, split the band etched near the knuckle.

Her slippered feet swell, too. Unpredictable boat-blocks, they hold
inside one move, nothing swing, nothing called *fox,* just one blue bee-

line, dreadful and straight. We take her wrist and crowd the bed
and we encircle her—ghost of leanness, muscle blown, skin

no more tissue than wind. This serum is serious and mean.

—*Open Competition Winner*

Barbara Buckman Strasko

Solo in the Snow

The trumpet player wants to teach his son jazz,

so one night he takes him out to the dusted white ground,

lays his bare hand against the cold and makes

angels, and a sun, carves an owl
and figures that have no recognizable form,

draws long lines and short gestures. Then he
makes a crescent moon that

reflects the light falling onto the earth—
he does all of this—

then erases it with the broom from the snowman's hand.

—*Open Competition Winner*

Adam Chiles

In Passing

Inside, a spore of light settles on the narrow pew.
Hole of God, our Lord's socket.

What beak drilled this lidless peep?
What starving rook labored at the ceiling?

All winter, this diminutive coin
of light, this holy farthing.

My mother lingering by the keys, her feet
underneath, cycling the organ pedals. She is the only hymn

for miles. Her feet sew
the injured notes, paddling them

into a silent hull
of air. As she plays, history makes room

for her, and this fragment,
this brief ascension into the chapel loft

is enough. Nearly eighty. Everything she knows
and does not know spindles here

momentarily, her carefully scripted hair,
its silvering bun. Her feet though,

buoyant, weighing their music back into the clotted pipes.
What god leans an eye or ear to this?

What tiny mote drifts behind her, warming
the empty celestial pew?

And who will place a collection dish under this light?
Who will bow at this dry font,

breathe what is here.

—Open Competition Winner

Gary Joseph Cohen

Bibliotalpidae

There was a period of time
When skulking on all fours

Along the stream to the library
Filled my mind with filthy ideas

About loose-leaf and leather tooling, and
More often for roots than affixes

You could find me brushing my velvet
Legs against cracked and dusty spines,

Eyes recessed, hands tunneling between stacks
With my head cocked and arms raised,

Mouth working over the plates,
Tongue deep in thought with a hair

Between my blond teeth, lids and fingers
At peace among rhizomes,

At peace among bookworms and earwigs,
At peace with digging and clawing

Through the fly leaves and torn jackets,
The library blinds drawn for sedition,

The doors open for secrecy.

—Open Competition Winner

Dina Hardy

Vol. L, Pg. 4242, from The World Book

Fire and night are held in the skull.
Melted fat, lit rushes and bone:
the first lamp. Capillary attraction of the wick
(the sticks) for the grease, keeps the flame
burning. For twenty-seven years, Webster wrote

the first American dictionary by candle,
light reflected off highly polished tin.
Before this, *music* ended with a 'k.'
Now the 'u' is lost in *color*. Paint
and printer's ink came from crude lampblack

(see: soot). At the bottom of the ocean,
the lamprey, lowest of vertebrates,
possibly the ancient ancestor of all animals
with backbones, attaches its teeth to fish,
scrapes a hole in the flesh, and sucks

out blood. Death from diseases
like rheumatic fever or mathematics,

the recurrence of certain numbers. 42
is 21 doubled, which is 12 mirrored. This page
repeats 42 twice. 2+3+7=12. Room 237

is the room in *The Shining* where
the lights stay on. Stay away. Spine:
appendages of bone, the hinged back
of a book, shiver down the.
It's All Forgotten Now is the 13th song

on this LP soundtrack. Electricity replaced kerosene
replaced oils replaced candles replaced
grease. The Guttenberg Printing Press,
next typewriters. 9-to-5's are now 8-to-6.
All work and no play. . . Burning the midnight,

the candle. . . the ash at the end of a cigarette
doesn't drop during a long take under blazing
studio lights (see: sun lamp). A fire
reduced the set to cinders. *Cut* for the night,
for morning keeps gold in its mouth.

—*Open Competition Winner*

Anna Journey

Lucifer's Panties at Lowe's Garden Center

I told the serial killer he could feed his Venus flytrap Spam
         the summer I worked the outdoor lawn

and garden center. I'd known to say this since fifteen, with my mother telling me
         all men who ask young girls directions
from their white vans are murderers. Especially ones

wearing an arm in a sling who ask you to carry things. This one asked about hibiscus.
         I said *Rum Runner, the Fifth Dimension, Eye of the Storm.*

The flower with my own name, *Anna Elizabeth,* was too damn pink and ruffled. I switched
         its label, wrote *Lucifer's Panties,* stuck its white plastic
flag back. I named others *Unquenchable Burning, Hellflames,*

Fire on the Back of Your Dark Tongue. He wanted instead to apologize
         with the crepe-yellow hybrid for a woman

whose dining room window he'd shattered with a corner of drywall. He asked
         if the gift was a good idea. I told him he was going to need
a good pot—one with an angel,

copper frog, fat gnome, or fairy: *Girls love that shit.* Probably terracotta.

His slung arm—likely struck by lightning from handling Bluebeard's hoard
        on the aluminum bed of his construction van.
I helped him repot. The killer grasping the flowers' pale trumpets, me

tamping the dark roots. Before he left, a turnip moth

played the wind chimes above the register without touching them.
        I pointed to the label, *direct sun,* but couldn't say:

bring the blooms indoors before the frost.

—Nominated by Virginia Commonwealth University

Christina Mengert

Apology

Years later, the sun does nothing to itself but burn. Consider the facts:
One shoe is independent of the sun. One thing stares at the other,
And in doing so allows it, in turn, to see. Another shoe, tossed up,
Ignites. Your sun is the first and foremost operative in this illusion.
On any given day it is a numeral. How like a world to describe itself
In a way only it can understand, to look at light and bind it to function.
I see through the glass, see only white and stop. See you and stop.
The sun blackens, offers irises on the flat of a wide silver platter.
You take them in twos, eyes directed at the face of it not rising but blocked
By another body. Turning from you, I press my face into the window.
The sun does nothing but burn, I say, pulling petals from our eyes.
You exchange them for those kept in hand since I first ventured close.
Admit before now they have gone unread.

—Nominated by the University of Denver

Quinn Latimer

Chekhov's Photograph

I.

It's awful how easily women give
themselves away to men, said my friend,
to whom I had given myself away

twice. I was in the middle of the second
terrible giving when he said this. Outside
car alarms began in sharp chorus: *no, no, no.*

His face turning to ember busied itself
with distance. Feeling my way through
the air, I sat at the small, scarred piano

that sulked near the window. Thought of only
the feral cats rubbing up against the stucco
of his house, the awful orange claw of their bodies.

Virginia Woolf said of Chekhov:
"We must cast about to find out
where in these stories the emphasis lies."

The cats, etc. Yes or no. No. The mock
irony of his understanding (yes) and the attendant
instrument (no). Desire stuttering out of the room (perhaps).

I once searched Chekhov's photograph for what
was most emphatically *him:* turned-
up collar of the narrow double-breasted

coat, puckered poof of sleeves, the fore-
finger of his right hand resting lightly
on a thin, shiny cane. Leaning back easily

on an elbow, his eyes pressed into me.
On the porch behind, an empty chair
sat awkwardly above him, as though it were

a painting intimidated by its owner. He was
a sharp dresser, that Doctor. His kind eyes,
they pecked at my face. We do not always want

understanding. It can also be a form of betrayal. For instance:
In a dream I have over and over, my mother
and I rest on the roof of a house in the middle

of a turquoise sea. As the rip begins to pull
me out to where the water is darker, she must
swim me in. The house's strict minimalism

infers my fear of enclosure (perhaps), but could also
mean my love of the lines. Waking from this dream,
shame is always what dresses me. And this might be

the emphasis, yes? Not the salt that streaks her arms.
My mother has always said that I hang on
too long. That in this way, I am like my father.

II.

In the story where Woolf lost her footing at
"a long gray fence studded with nails," I was struck
by Chekhov's understanding of Gurov:

"He always seemed to women different
from what he was, and they loved in him not
himself, but the man whom their imagination

created and whom they had been seeking
all their lives; and afterwards, when they saw
their mistake, they loved him nevertheless.

And not one of them had been happy with him."
I say *struck* deliberately, because, as after
a slap, I was left with that burning sensation

coupled with a feeling of ice. Gurov found love
with "The Lady with the Pet Dog," but why?
And she, Anna, was not happy with him,

but like those women before her, she did not
seek him for happiness. She sought him for love.
But what made her love real and not

a creation of her imagination? Was his love for her
simply his imagination come suddenly loose,
like some steamer off Yalta released from its pier

and set adrift into fog, and so into wild, terrible
being? These are very elementary questions, but
they interest me. When one is left alone

in love, these questions become important.
Behind my friend's house, where I sat tracing
wet-glass rings on a piano, an alley glittered of glass,

catching the light from a sunset that had dropped
its red cape over the desert basin of the city. It was
Chekhov's demonstration that Gurov's new

and fuller understanding of himself and Anna
had come only with his love for her, that worried
me. True knowledge of oneself and others

can take place outside of love. The doubleness
of understanding that Chekhov located within love—
as Gurov understood that, for him, there was no human

more important in the world than Anna, this little,
provincial woman—also occurs outside of it.
For instance, sitting there in my friend's room,

as he circled me with his new wash of remove,
his understanding parsing my brain into
unrelated fragments, I also saw us both quite clearly.

III.

It was like standing outside a small corral,
and watching a horse circle its perimeter
over and over, the sound of hooves in canter

coming closer, becoming harsh, and then
receding, and then again. When the horse
suddenly stops, nostrils flared and breathing hard,

the heat discernible in the dust that fills the air,
and then spins into the opposite direction
and begins its circling anew, one knows the change

of direction will occur before the horse ever
slides to a stop. Because watching from
the perimeter, one cannot help but be the horse

as well as oneself. The understanding does not come
from love always. It can come from proximity.
My friend, my lover, began to circle closer,

seeing in me, what? Himself (perhaps). Outside, the cats
began shrieking of the electricity of their bodies.
Words made tiny fists (yes) inside my mouth.

—*Nominated by* Seneca Review

Eduardo C. Corral

Se Me Olvidó Otra Vez

after Donald Justice

I sit in bed, from the linen your scent still rises.
You're asleep inside your old guitar.

A mariachi suit draped on a chair, its copper buttons,
the eyes of jaguars stalking the night.

I sit in bed, from the linen your scent still rises.

Through a window a full moon brings to mind Borges,
there is such loneliness in that gold.

You're asleep inside your old guitar.

Are your calloused heels scraping its curved wood or
are there mice scurrying in the walls?

I sit in bed, from the linen your scent still rises.

I flick on a lamp, yellow light strikes your guitar
like dirt thrown on a coffin.

You're asleep inside your old guitar.
I sit in bed, from the linen your scent still rises.

—Open Competition Winner

Susan Settlemyre Williams

Lighter

> *The sparks scatter everywhere...they flutter about in the movements*
> *of the world, searching where they can lodge to be set free.*
> —Martin Buber

1. Zippo

Spark, pull toward the mouth
of small steady flame. Pale lipstick (Frosted Glow)
creped on a filtertip. My monogrammed Zippo,

twelfth-grade Christmas gift from my best friend,
in my pocket when we were caught
discussing her pregnancy over cigarettes

in the restroom before graduation. Lost
sometime that summer—one of many bright
things I've had and can't remember when they left

my possession. Love letters, jewelry. My friend,
the other Susan, who knew when she lost
the baby—smoke rings

we taught ourselves to make, sprawled
on her mother's couch, while her father's last
Jack Daniels paled in our melting ice. Spark, then smoke.

2. *Fatwood*

Lighter wood, my grandmother called it,
fatwood, resin-stiff splinters of pine tempered
by fire—one spark and they catch. The loblolly

by my window didn't catch when lightning
gouged a channel last night and flung
wet pulp in ribbons onto my stoop.

But the sparks wait in everything now;
inside the bark, resin boiled, distilled
to lighter-wood pitch, ready next time to flare.

3. *Becoming Light*

At dawn the air skitters. Particles
of light trapped in the almost-dark,
colliding. When they find each other,
they slow down. It's daylight.

Light on dandelions shatters
the globes. The filaments lift, floss
of milkweed lifts. They rise all day on heat,

and we never see the fall, its finality,
plunging seed through a crack in clay,
fattening into taproot.

Without the stone in her belly, Susan
lifted, lost as dandelion silk
in a milky sky. It was not
a matter of joy.

4. The Breaking of the Vessels

The universe began when God miscalculated, pouring god-light into vessels of light,
and they broke. God broke. Primordial error, before Eden, before serpent and fruit
and Eve mouthing the word sin and thinking *how will anything happen if I don't
know the taste of it?* The breaking set everything in motion, necessitated the world of
matter: breeding ground for the good, who are born to gather up and raise the
sparks that scattered into chaos, into dark everything. Their mitzvoth, says Luria,
joining all the lost light, will make God whole again.

5. Spark to Smoke

Centuries wore down my grandmother's house
into particles of light. The lightning

found it in sudden recognition—spark
and flame. They saved a chest,

a desk, lockbox of old deeds. The spoons
and drawer pulls melted to lumps, glass

ran in a river under the cinders and sank
out of memory. Like darkness

between the sparks of cigarettes that night
we finished the bottle Susan's father left her

when he shot himself and nothing
connected light to light but our smoke, rising.

—Open Competition Winner

Elizabeth Bradfield

Cul-de-sac Linguistics

Today, the boys call each other penis.
Hey penis, commere, penis, pass me the ball,
penis. Last week it was whore, discovered

halfway through a game of h o r s e
on the mini-hoop that backs my fence.
And earlier this afternoon, the teenage girls

whose bedroom window stares
above my thumbnail yard improvised
outgoing messages in theatrical rapture:

first the easy scatological, then
a nursery rhyme that morphs
into an anti-homo riff so suddenly

I actually look up

to see if they're directing this at me
(they must be), down in the yard, reading poetry
as my girlfriend weeds the flower bed.

O, the high profanity of kickball games,
the rough posturing demanded
by even this tame street. Listen, they're learning

how well bastard fits with fucking, how ass
can't be misused. No one could hope to ease
their jagged entries into this profane world

which is fucking beautiful, ass-bastard gorgeous,
the evening light wild and soaring
like kickballs on a true arc into flowerbeds

of penis tulips and pussy daffodils
that nod their heads in wild agreement
with the whorish, shit-loving lot of it.

—Open Competition Winner

Julie Larios

Double Abecedarian: Please Give Me....

Anything & anybody but Freud, that Bic-and-Pez-
Bitten, cylinder-obsessed, Big-Cigar-As-Envy
Calamity of a man who posited the idea that sex
Dachshund-style with mom might possibly show
Evidence of a troubled mind. How did every concave *V*
Female its way into his convex psyche? *Mon dieu,*
Gott im himmel, por el amor de dios—just one night
How I'd like to translate myself without the shrinks.
I wouldn't get lost in fog, I wouldn't be a beggar
Jumping off the Pont Neuf, wouldn't be a twisted *Q*
Knocking up some *U* with my tail, nor a Lap-
Lander hitching myself to my own sled. No,
More likely I'd just be sitting looking for a reason
Not to stop sitting. There'd either be me in this dream,
Or some smoke and some midgets. Does all hell
Position itself for a couched session with that sick
Quill-and-quiver-addled Viennese? He's still the Raj
Royale of our subsurfaces, isn't he, the Rabbi
Sigmund ben Oedipus? He makes even bowls of mush
Turn into latent tendencies, while we keep cranking
Up his sirens without any downtime or relief.

Virility as a red fire hydrant, lust as a long flagpole?
Where on this earth, or where off it, do these bad
X-rated verticalities escape from his narrative arc?
Yes, the shapes of this world go from arrow to orb,
Zero is a pierced hole. But what a lot of hoopla.

—*Nominated by* The Georgia Review

Stephanie Rogers

Symphony for Red

All the red has been used up and buttoned
across the backs of butterflies and crowned
     upon the new-hatched cardinal's head, the red
unfurling feathers streaked with heat as bright
     as August sun and dark as cherry stems.
I've touched the broken checkmarks, zigged and zagged
     inside a tired eyeball—ant farms—red
and mean as fire, pulsing up like armies
     digging from a poison-threatened pupil,
the iris, optic nerve, and redder still
     the broken vessels near the nose's bridge.
They curl like forgotten threads dropped to the floor,
     a sewing kit gone mad with bleeding spools.
Even the scattered sky flags down the day
     with a red-tinged hat removed and flicked, a signal,
a shake of crimson here and there and *there,*
     beside the wide-mouthed cat greeting the dawn.
But gone, an hour later. Instead—a blind-
     slat scar of yellow sunlight peeking through.
And gone—the vacuumed threads, the cardinal
     who unpacked the earth, its morning search for life—

a slithering meal. Like that. Just gone, a dash
     of rose across a cheek, a faded smack,
the starry flint of a cigarette alive
     on a lawn and left to scorch inside a hiss
of rain. Then back again—so soon—as rain
     begins the deeper stain of petals, bricks,
illuminates the stoplights, stop signs, red
     against the paint-chipped red that still, that *still*
exists even in dark. And then, a spark
     of light, the clouds gathered like a thumping heart,
a spilling bowl of strawberries, then gone—
     Like that—erotic sky turned gray and calm,
a vanished anger, quick to blur, dismissed
     and absent still: your skin, your hands, your lips,
all gone—and weren't *they* red?

—*Open Competition Winner*

Jaimee Hills

Still Life

When they unearthed my body, I was precious,
not for my pretty sapphires, which I lacked,
but because life lay still in me. Precautions
were taken to keep me there; I'd been locked,
this form in a coffin, but I'd been licked
and pried open. Theirs was a loathsome practice,
I thought, burgling the dead to steal peace.
I'd rot soon enough without some precocious
anatomist cutting me up to display me on his lectern.
This man walked the length of my hand, punctured
my skin, hurried down to the quiet heart, located
my female parts. He emptied me like a pitcher,
a pretty little teapot, pretty as a picture.
His hands began to map a chart of living, looked
through me, learning, while my insides leaked out.
He arranged my organs like fruit in a dish, all pinkish,
sketched me quickly. Now my body lies likened
in a manuscript. I'd lived on. I'd lucked out.
What great things I could do besides perish.

—Open Competition Winner

Gaynell Gavin

Remembering the Bear

Our company commander loved
his orphaned Rocky Mountain black bear
cub more than he loved us. The cub grew up.
His Quang Tri bunker—theoretically
air-conditioned to satisfy
the SPCA before we left Fort Carson,
except the generator wouldn't work in Viet Nam—

that bunker was still better than ours,
which pissed us off, but we always said hi
anyway to Brutus T. Bear.

From our bunker, we saw across the DMZ,
to the red and gold NVA flag. Brutus helped us
interrogate NVA soldiers. Then he got sick,
and neither the Con Thien battalion surgeon
or the one flown from Da Nang especially
for the occasion could save him. We caved
his bunker in over him to bury him in Viet Nam.

—Open Competition Winner

Drew Blanchard

Idle

On weeknights my father disappeared
into his windowless shed with a bottle of Schlitz
and boxes from Frank's Salvage and Junk.
From fifteen broken watches he'd make
two whole again—with radios and cameras
it took twenty or thirty to get one—his gifts
for birthdays and Christmases. My brother and I
begged to help, but the closed shed door
repeated his no. We only saw the remains
of this strange world—forty-six radios,
thirty watches, and ten cameras shelved
above mountains of gears and wires.
"Leave it all," he said, when his legs failed
and we sold the house. Now he has passed
from even his final, tiny room;
but the city he built in this retired idle time
is still spread across the mahogany hutch
but now in my study. He willed this toy train,
his hours of building to me, left a note
taped to the caboose in his sideways scrawl:

"you can give it to your boy,
and let him blow the damn whistle."

—Open Competition Winner

Lisa Gluskin

Spring Forward

A hot day and a woodpecker carves away
at backyard aspen, the dog's ear swiveling
like a tiny satellite dish: pinpoint,
lock on. Morning and the neighborhood
rotates around that point, springing taut
toward equinox. Little flashes call out to those
who can read their language but glitter
for everyone, the planet an ear in a swirl of sound.

In one photograph teletype operators
sit at the alert, collars buttoned high, each finger
rearing back over a single shining key,
each key lit from behind: lone lamppost
spilling glint across filigree and pomade,
skimming even wrought iron with a sheen
of pale sand. Sending it outward,
out here where we keep our images mobile.

That lost hour went somewhere, surely—
out there ready to bank back home
one October midnight, deeper into this
flattened century. Some half-full moon
of the future, and under it a wind-up bird.

—*Nominated by* Michigan Quarterly Review

James Crews

Foreshadowing

> *I don't mind winter because I know*
> *what follows. There are laws.*
> —Belle Waring

Snow clouds fill the sky
like a power you never knew
you had. The man next to you
on this rush hour bus
who has stuffed plastic bags
into the holes of his coat
huddles close to look out
your window as if the sunset
might burst for once with the red
of alpenglow, as if these piles
of snow were only beginnings
of mountains trying to rise up.
But you know the cold and ice
will give up these plains again
as a robe gives up the body
underneath. Color always
returns, if slowly, to the earth

like the self you thought
you already were all winter.

—*Nominated by The University of Wisconsin-Madison*

Christopher Cunningham

Mr. Robinson at the Supermarket

Recently, he stopped doing his own shopping.
Unpacking groceries made him unbearably sad.
The bags were too full of things he already knew,

so he decided to let other people
choose his food for him. The man in Produce
sent him to the Customer Service Desk,

where the Assistant Manager smiled, shrugged,
apologized. He nodded and pushed his empty basket
toward the back of the store, where in the cereal aisle

he found an unattended shopping cart
full of food and shuffled to the checkout.
In the evenings after dinner, he sits

at his kitchen table and thinks about things.
For example, organic deodorant,
beets, baby food, feminine hygiene,

unscented anti-static dryer-towelettes.
For example, the woman across the hall
and her nine cats, each named for one of the planets;

his Japanese Maple bonsai, whose tiny branches
toss and quake with his breath; his goldfish, whose mouth
endlessly forms and re-forms the slow shape

of a question he can never quite hear.

—Open Competition Winner

J.M. Hughes

Tongue: Variations

1. Elocution Lessons at the Cotillion

The goal is restraint: each tongue,
tethered by nylon string
like the trunks of fruit trees,
anchored to correct their leanings.

The object is to avoid dissonance,
each tongue striking like a plectrum
against the backs of square teeth,
they all arrive at a perfect 't.'

Each tongue, indiscernible from the next;
the desks lined up in orchard rows.
Carefully repeat the following words:
Yes. Please. Thank You. Pardon me.

Mozart plays harpsichord. We practice
passing the tea tray to a waltz.
We watch with the delicate fear
that comes with cultivation and breeding.

2. Native Tongue: The Other Pentecost

The maize rows went
one by one, withered ears
leapt up, tongues of flame
lapped at noonday skies,
at bodies huddled
against umber earth.

In my memory,
all is slow motion:
on the ground, a woman
burning, her wide hips
propelling her body
back and forth
to put the flames out.

Her hips, that rhythm,
were all she had,
a *Filomena*
with her tongue cut out
by a soldier's serrated knife.
No one speaks of her.
No one speaks for her.

So, each night I try
to approximate
the rhythm of those hips
with my tongue.
In the middle of the night,

my ululations bring trains
to a grinding halt.

3. Origins

Hyoid bone: calcium and phosphorous.
Muscle: blood and fiber.
Blood and muscle: vehicles of rhythm.

4. Faculties

Taste: salt, iron, sugar, carbon (see blood, *def. d*).
Speech: three basic functions: praise, blame, petition.
Idiom or Language: unstable bridge between individuals.

5. My Tongue

for Rhett Poché

works in solitude;
stealing words
from the ghosts
that have settled in
worn pages, or
the mortar between
the bricks of ruined houses
in abandoned lots.

But, for you
I improvise, carrying
my own words
across this bridge of flesh
in a single breath.
I extend my tongue
in surrender to yours,
to bury the dead
for the love of living.

—*Nominated by University of Notre Dame*

Amanda Auchter

The Catherine Wheel

after St. Catherine of Alexandria

Wish for the stone to fall away from the wrist
that throws it.   That it lands outside
the shadow-

curve my head casts. Wind-knocked
into a grain barrel,

or caught in the teeth
of the wheel. Ripped into bark, a wound.

Firework that spins as it burns. Let this

turn break the tree that binds my mouth
to its splinter. In this square

of voices—each mother covers
her child's head with her
palms as though they cannot hear

my mouth open and close. How my bones
               stumble into the blind

river, each break a light passing
through. Ask of death:

                   where is there to go?

The fist of God is too small for me to hide.
Let me set like a loom, let the birds

take each eye skyward. By the time
             the children look, there are no eyes,

no wheel, not blood, but milk.

                   —*Open Competition Winner*

Karen Lepri

Pilgrimage

Each time they sought a darker eye
for snacks and sex with strangers;
how they stopped along the way
in Venice, in Byzantium,
a new brand of heretic
a more queer prayer.

This is to know disappointment:
to follow Peter,
to leave sanctity.
If only they had known
that Jerusalem's walls had purpose

but after scaling them,
but after the massacre,
the smell of rot and Muslim blood
was enough to hang the pilgrims
with doubt, to drag them
thirsty, to the edge of the saltiest sea.

—Open Competition Winner

Brian Leary

Self-Portrait as Suicide Girl's Skirt

First, the pleats fell in love with each other.
Each blind edge bent its knees & bared teeth

like a horse. Whoever's blinked once between words,
whoever's unfurled a face & promised to love,
knows not enough was said
but really
not enough to say.

Stop heavy horsy, he said. Says. *Stop*
clanging your metal feet. I've tried to bite through myself,

one open end to the other. Fell through stitches & prayed.
Stop. I do. I keep still, let
a whisper pull out through the vault of my skull.

I do not frighten myself anymore.
I feel the hothouse push of spring. In my chest,
a small girl is sobbing & I know
to buy her a wig of woolen yarn.

—*Open Competition Winner*

Jay Nebel

The Romantic

I've been to the movie about the flood where the boy and girl float
under the latticed bridges, miraculously still, their bodies only touching
from elbow to wrist, and somehow, they stay together
amidst the wreckage of refrigerators and station wagons,
soggy stuffed animals, wooden houses, eyeless dolls
and picket fences that drift through a city, held together tenderly
as the ash of a cigarette. They survive, get married,
live happily for six months, never fight, make love
on the kitchen tile, until one morning a water logged greeting card
shows up on their doorstep, a heart felt fuck you
scratched on the inside. We find out he has cancer, only one day
to live, and we feel cheated as they spend the last hours feeding
the ducks on Laurelhurst Pond, because we have to return
to our ordinary lives, snapping you bare ass with a wet towel
on Halloween, or you splitting my lip months earlier
in a wrestling match. Or leaving me standing there
in a Home Depot parking lot wondering if you would ever
come back with our two Chihuahuas and the new barbecue loaded
into the backseat of the car, pissed because I paid too much attention

to the cashier, my marriage driving away with her hands
on the wheel, music blasting, the wind smashing her in the face.

—Nominated by the University of Oregon

John W. Evans

Zugzwang

> *(n.) "Compulsion to move." A chess term referring*
> *to a situation in which a player would like to do*
> *nothing (pass), since any move will damage his position.*

Not that it mattered in the beginning
but there were patterns. I saw three moves
to your bishop, six to your rook, nine to your queen
and then a slow game of pawns. Almost at mate,
I forgot the axes running to the corners,
failed to anticipate your casual sweep of the lanes,
one side of my board plucked clean like a branch of wild
anything. You opened a window to let out the heat.
We started again. It felt good to keep playing,
to do one thing well over and over again.
Maybe that's why I liked
the pizza place around the block that burnt our crusts,
why you could not wait to move uptown,
away from the martinis, mochas, and Marc Jacobs.
Our new home was several blocks from anywhere.
Half a mile out the buoy lights shined like rosary beads.

If we were quiet and mindful the trees around the lake
shook when we walked beneath them.

—Nominated by Florida International University

Natalie Shapero

Nymphet

Already, she's the smallest she can be;
the suffix is superfluous as froth.
She's reached the apotheosis of appearing
as though she incubated in a lily
that swooned its petals open to give birth.
No second syllable, no clever tack
could make her nutshell river raft more real,
nor more insistent her slim finger's crook.

And yet we have a word that does just that.
That's progress for you, people: someone teased
and praised and scared that little syllable
until she spun on ribboned ankles, fell,
and told herself she loved the fall so much,
she paid to have its portrait done in oil.

I've spun, myself; he used to use a strap
to fasten me inside the giant ball
that whirled at zero gravity. He'd feed
me after: freeze-dried fries. He used to play
me Mozart like I was the favored fern

in a science project. Graphs were drafted. Notes
were taken. He talked about me all the time.
I thought I'd like to get a big bass drum
with my name on it. But *which* name, I would wonder.
He calls me lots of things. He calls me Champ
and Slugger, says I do so good at what
I do. He calls me Runt. (I'm small.) He calls
me Baby Nova, Beamface, Pint-o'-Stars.
I burst. He calls me Artist, and I paint
a sunset on my face. But those are names
you'd never know were mine. No, when he talks
to anyone but me, he calls me low,
calls low and calls me lowly, *lo-li,* calls
me by his favorite nickname
                 for Dolores.

                      —*Nominated by* 32 Poems

Heather June Gibbons

Muse the Drudge

I, hackneyed beauty queen cut
With kitchen knife, whir, tilt off

Spin fast, a heavy eddy, I am no
Girl-wisp, nor clipped wingtip

Nor treachery of baubles, nor branded
By word, nor shut up in a cave

No-body, no birdie, I leak, call me
Sheela-na-gig, Astarte, Dora, cheap

Whiskey in cut-crystal, watch it your
Earlobe's in my teeth, I blow shit up

Heart-husk, wax drip, I lick you, there
Now you're licked. I, twitchy harlot

I, muse the drudge, poison cup, slipknot
Not precious, not spread, here, hold it

To your ear, hear me laughing
I, kitten-heeled, do drop kick

I, I, I, beget, taste, hang by threads
Of smoke, I cloy, my mouth drips

Venery, I weave my own shroud,
Burn ink, and dare you, speak of me.

—Open Competition Winner

Meg Shevenock

This Could Be It

> *The time of all forgotten / Things is at hand.*
> —John Ashbery

The orange-cream kitten crying outside our door,
we ignored on the grounds that we, too,

felt unfulfilled. I try not to picture the disintegrating fur
of its ribs, the tiny, oblong cage sinking into the mulch under the house.

I have begun collecting screen doors
from junkyards, lining them along the deck, pressing

my face against the iron-flavored air. *Why sit all day outside,*
you say, *and act as though you're in, longing to be outside?*

You hurry in white pants down the steps
to paint houses. You're like a character in a movie

with your to-do lists and hot coffee from the deli.
You believe there's something more, that I don't get it, but I do.

Behind your back I collect other things too—
lately, the black plastic combs photographers

hand out to children on school-picture day. Pressing the teeth
of one into my palm, I'm reminded of looking in a mirror

in a dim room over the Allegheny, of the pale corner of my mother's mouth,
or the last stretch of field in our town. Everything I bring in

is anchored to another memory I don't own.
We choose our separate sides of the house and pray.

—Nominated by the University of Florida

Maud Kelly

For the Man Who Threw Himself from the Building

Unfortunately, it was beautiful
to watch you in your suit
erase the sky, lift all sound away.
Everything else became not you.
I am sorry to hold you like this—
bury you, dig you up again.
I wish I could smudge you into something else,
something my mother would like—
a spark coming off a campfire,
winking as it rises,
or a calligraphy, the character
for husband (man leaving the house)
or faith (prisoner lifting the latch)—
but you are always, and I,
I remember this:
My uncle, on a crisp fall day,
threw a red boomerang against the blue.
It hurtled off, clung a moment
to the hem of sky's loose coat,
then came back and back and back.

—Open Competition Winner

Andrew Kozma

Elegy for the End of the World

> In 1923, in Vyatka Prison, the SR Struzhinsky and his comrades
> (how many were there? who were they? what were they protest-
> ing against?) barricaded themselves in a cell, poured kerosene
> over all the mattresses and *incinerated themselves.*
> —Aleksandr I. Solzhenitsyn, *The Gulag Archipelago*

When the second hand stops, a sudden rainstorm
pauses, holds itself like snow on the television screen,
in each drop the burst of flame's reflection
from another angle becomes a street on fire.

Kerosene is blessed with this: it tastes like whiskey
as it burns your throat, and the air stinks sweetly
that smokes from your mouth. But this no one will know
but you, and you are quickly becoming that air.

There are no relatives, no pictures, nothing
but a bright plume in the distance, centered
over the city and blowing closer. It is night.
It is day. The clouds will wear your face.

—Open Competition Winner

Theo Hummer

Embalm

1. These truths are difficult to reconcile.
2. The heel, though designed to resist injury, heals very slowly; the jelly eye heals fast.
3.

Montana is	Montana is a	Montana is
where one man	place and	noplace
however huge	one huge man	and one human
is noplace,	is noplace,	is nothing,
lost inside of it.	lost inside of it.	lost inside of it.

4. *Sssss*—dogs pissing, dusk. As I pass I see pale walls, room bare of furniture. Ammonia outdraft, melancholy. Etched into the sidewalk: *God rules. Die, Mr. Squirrel!* Homeless people have set up lawn furniture outside Walgreen's. That fence-climbing night—the hills—eucalyptus shadows falling on our hair: plum trees laden, Mexican sage, goldfish ponds, cast-iron children's furniture and in the one, a little fountain—dogs. Concrete dogs pissing.
5. I cannot care to be industrious.
6. balm, *n* [ME *baume;* OFr *basme;* L *balsamum,* from Gr *balsamon,* balsam] 1. an aromatic gum resin obtained from certain trees and used as a medicine. 2. any fragrant ointment or aromatic oil for healing or anointing. 3. anything which heals, soothes, or mitigates pain or mental distress.
7. Messages of hope must be cryptic or readers may become jealous, suspecting your life easier than theirs.

1. The eye, then even the heel.
2. The sequence of my thoughts is different in this air, this place, time passing.
3. balm, *n* [Sans.] 1. an invocation used by the Hindus in worship in the form either of a brief petition or of the repetition of a sacred word. 2. a hymn of praise contained in the Vedas. 3. anything which heals, soothes, or mitigates pain or mental distress.
4. *Sssss*—dogs at dusk. Through the window I can see blue walls, room bare but for a photo, hung, framed. Outdraft of ammonia cleanser. Still homeless. Etched into the sidewalk: *God rules. Die, Mr. Squirrel!*—under a layer of fallen, rain-soaked leaves. Make a list of those who know it's there. Remember this: we climbed fences—swanky hills—eucalyptus on our faces, our combined hair. Plums, sage, goldfish, cast iron and the little fountain—dogs. Concrete dogs pissing on the gardens of California.
5. These truths are difficult to reconcile.
6. A binary star's members revolve around their common center of gravity.
7. Montana   Montana   Montana
   is a place   is a huge place   is a huge place
   and one human   and one man   and one man
   is nothing,   is nothing, lost   is nothing lost
   lost inside of it. inside of it.   inside of it.

—Nominated by Sentence

William Ashley Johnson

Survey

for Ruth

We walk what might be your brother's land,
moving from stake to stake,
their pink plastic blooms an unnatural line
beneath the scrub pine and second growth.
Ferried and fed for our opinion
when we speak though, it is of *our* acreage,
how wind crosses the mountain,
where the sun would rise and set,
best views and neighbors.

From one plot to the next our words carve and clear,
performing the heavy lifting of making the land lay,
until only the churchless hilltop cemetery remains.

Over the chained cattle gate we find corralled
headstones and butterflies, enough for each its own,
and not a flower to be seen.
The crisp lines of the swallowtail's yellow and black
move in erratic flight above the steady, even rows of tired slabs,

and render a reckoning exact
and an image perhaps too perfect for the page.

Here again, is our home, plot and parcel.
In that place between
so many beating wings and worn stone,
is only you and I, another benchmark,
offering an orientation all its own.

—Open Competition Winner

Jill Osier

Bedful of Nebraskas

I go out and bring flowers in.
Everyone does, no one questions it.
Bouquet of greed, of dread, you
are dead as the black stump in the pasture
that every so often stretches its neck,
trying to be a horse. We give things names
to stop the spinning; we call it love
when we agree. That is a garage, this, tired,
this, how far the trees look when it's snowing.
Now the other six come over the hill as if for water.
The black horse has finally stood and they're cheering him on,
rearing and fearing they are the only horses for miles.

—Nominated by Black Warrior Review

Contributors' Notes

DEBORAH AGER's writing has appeared in *The Georgia Review, New England Review, New Letters, The North American Review, Quarterly West,* and elsewhere. She has been awarded fellowships at the MacDowell Colony, the Virginia Center for the Creative Arts and the Jenny McKean Moore Workshop. She's the founding publisher and editor of *32 Poems Magazine.*

ANDREW ALLPORT is currently completing a Ph.D. in English and creative writing at the University of Southern California, where he teaches literature and composition. The poem "An Unknown Shore" begins with a series of three unpublished fragments from the notebooks of George Oppen.

AMANDA AUCHTER is the editor of *Pebble Lake Review* and the author of the chapbook *Light Under Skin* (Finishing Line Press, 2006). She is the recipient of the 2005 Milton Kessler Memorial Poetry Prize from *Harpur Palate* and the 2005 James Wright Poetry Award from *Mid-American Review.* Her poetry appears in *Born Magazine, Columbia Poetry Review, Crab Orchard Review,* and elsewhere.

TERESA BALLARD's poems have appeared or are forthcoming in: *Massachusetts Review, Mid-American Review, Pleiades, Poetry Northwest, The Drunken Boat, Comstock Review, Paumanok Review, Tryst, Three Candles,* as well as other literary journals. In December of 2005, she was a finalist for the *Mid-American Review's* James Wright Poetry Award. She has been nominated four times for the Pushcart Prize and is currently working on her first manuscript of poetry.

CIARAN BERRY received his M.F.A. from New York University, where he was awarded a *New York Times* fellowship, and where he currently teaches in the Expository Writing Program. His work has appeared most recently in *AGNI, The Threepenny Review, Green Mountains Review, The Southern Review, The Missouri Review,* and *The Ontario Review.* He is originally from the northwest of Ireland.

DREW BLANCHARD has studied at the University of Iowa and The Ohio State University. He is the author of the chapbook *Raincoat Variations* (Finishing Line Press, 2002) and his poems have appeared or are forthcoming in, among others, *Mudfish, Maize,* and *Notre Dame Review.*

ELIZABETH BRADFIELD lives in Anchorage, Alaska and works as a naturalist and Web designer. Her poems have appeared in *The Atlantic Monthly, Poetry, Field,* and *Bloom.* She is founder and editor of *Broadsided* (www.broadsidedpress.org).

JENNIFER CHAPIS was the 2005 recipient of the *Florida Review* Editor's Prize, and the *GSU Review* Poetry Prize judged by Thomas Lux. She has published poems with *Barrow Street, Hayden's Ferry Review, Hotel Amerika, Iowa Review, McSweeney's, Phoebe, Quarterly West,* and *Best New Poets 2005,* among others. An alumni of the Graduate Creative Writing Program at NYU, Jennifer is an editor with Nightboat Books (www.nightboat.org).

ADAM CHILES's work recently appeared in the following journals: *Arc, Barrow Street, The Beloit Poetry Journal, The Cimarron Review, Cue, Event, Indiana Review, Isotope, The Malahat Review, The New Delta Review, Nimrod International, The Oklahoma Review, Painted Bride Quarterly, Perihelion, Phoebe, Poet Lore, Prairie Fire, Prism International,* and *Smartish Pace.*

GARY JOSEPH COHEN's poems have appeared in *Parthenon West Review, Isotope Journal of Literary Nature and Science, New Orleans Review, Euphony, Best New Poets 2005,* and elsewhere. In 2005, Cohen received a Claudia Curfman Castellana Grant from The Calhoun School, where he teaches media arts, art history, and poetry, to travel to and experience first hand "earth works" sites around the American Southwest. He lives with his wife, Rebecca, and dog, Kozmo, in Manhattan.

EDUARDO C. CORRAL holds degrees from Arizona State Universtiy and the Iowa Writers' Workshop. His work has been recently honored with a Discovery/*The Nation* Award and a MacDowell Colony residency.

JAMES CREWS is originally from Saint Louis, Missouri. He now lives in Madison where he's completing his M.F.A. at the University of Wisconsin.

CHRISTOPHER CUNNINGHAM was educated at Stanford University and Duke University, where he received a Ph.D. in American literature. His poetry and criticism have appeared in *Iowa Review, Black Warrior Review, Ninth Letter, Mississippi Quarterly, Arizona Quarterly,* and elsewhere. His poetry manuscript *Uncanny Thirst* is available to an interested publisher. "Mr. Robinson at the Supermarket" is part of a new series of poems about Mr. Robinson and his peregrinations.

JOHN W. EVANS's poems have appeared in *Poetry East, Nimrod, 5AM, Harpur Palate, Epicenter,* and other magazines.

GAYNELL GAVIN's work has been published in such journals as *Prairie Schooner, The Comstock Review, Bellevue Literary Review, Quercus Review,* and *Tulane Review.* Her chapbook, *Intersections,* was published by Main Street Rag in 2005, and her memoir, *What I Did Not Say: Reflections of an Attorney-at-Large,* was a finalist for the 2003 AWP Award Series in Creative Nonfiction.

Originally from Bainbridge Island, Washington, HEATHER JUNE GIBBONS is an M.F.A. candidate in poetry at the Iowa Writers' Workshop. Her work has appeared or is forthcoming in *SHAMPOO, Cranky,* and *Third Coast.* In 2006, she attended the Prague Summer Program at Charles University as the Pavel Strut Poetry Fellow, was a finalist for the Indiana Review Poetry prize, and won a university award from the Academy of American Poets.

LISA GLUSKIN lives in San Francisco. After working as a magazine publisher, gift wrapper, film studio gofer, and cocktail waitress, she now makes her living as a freelance editor. Her poems have appeared in *Best New Poets 2005* and in journals such as *Michigan Quarterly Review, The Iowa Review, 32 Poems,* and *ZYZZYVA.* Lately she's been writing poems about theoretical cosmology and junior high school.

JESSICA GOODFELLOW's work has appeared in *Verse Daily, RATTLE, DIAGRAM,* and *Phoebe,* among other publications and Web sites, and she received the 2004 Chad Walsh Poetry Prize from the *Beloit Poetry Journal.* She has a chapbook forthcoming from Concrete Wolf and lives in Japan with her husband and two sons.

DINA HARDY's work has appeared or will appear in *Agni, Bellingham Review, Pool, Runes,* and *Smartish Pace.* She was a finalist for the *Poets & Writers* New Voices in California Contest. A recent graduate of the Iowa Writers' Workshop, she now lives in Burbank, California.

JAIMEE HILLS is the poetry, art, and comics editor of *Backwards City Review.* She received her M.A. in Writing Seminars at Johns Hopkins University and received her M.F.A. at the University of North Carolina at Greensboro, where she currently teaches writing and poetry.

Born and raised in Texas, J.M. HUGHES studied creative writing in New Orleans, Louisiana for four years before moving to South Bend, Indiana. In his spare time, he can be found composing music for piano, voice, or programming ambient electronica.

THEO HUMMER is a Ph.D. candidate at Cornell, where she also earned an M.F.A. in 2004. She co-curates the Soon poetry reading series in Ithaca, New York. Her poetry has appeared in *Sentence, Vox, Indiana Review,* and on the *Verse* magazine Web site.

WILLIAM ASHLEY JOHNSON was born and raised in Lexington, Kentucky and now lives in North Carolina with his wife, seven dogs, and three cats. He is an assistant poetry editor for the online journal *storySouth* (www.storysouth.com). His work has appeared in numerous journals, and his first book is forthcoming from Press 53 (www.press53.com) in the fall of 2007.

ANNA JOURNEY teaches creative writing at Virginia Commonwealth University, while completing her M.F.A. and serving as a contributing editor for *Blackbird*. She has received the 2005 *Sycamore Review* Wabash Prize for Poetry and the Academy of American Poets' Catherine and Joan Byrne Poetry Prize, among other awards. Her poetry appears or is forthcoming in *FIELD, Gulf Coast, Mid-American Review, Shenandoah,* and elsewhere. Her critical work appears in *Blackbird* and *Notes on Contemporary Literature.*

MAUD KELLY is an M.F.A. candidate at the University of Missouri-St. Louis and expects to graduate in May 2007.

PETER KLINE was a finalist for the 2004 Ruth Lilly Fellowship, and his poems have appeared in *Poetry, Best New Poets 2005, Smartish Pace, The Mississippi Review, Meridian, Cold Mountain, The Pinch,* and *Gulf Stream.*

ANDREW KOZMA attends the University of Houston for a Ph.D. in literature and creative writing while working as a non-fiction editor for *Gulf Coast*. His poems have appeared or are forthcoming in *Alehouse, Pebble Lake Review, Spoon River Poetry Review, Backwards City Review, Blue Mesa,* and *Forklift, Ohio*. He recently won the *Zone 3* Press First Book Award for his manuscript *City of Regret.*

JULIE LARIOS's poems have appeared in or are forthcoming in journals including *The Atlantic, The Georgia Review, The Threepenny Review, Ploughshares, FIELD, McSweeney's, Margie,* and *Prairie Schooner*. She is the winner of a Pushcart Prize and has work in this year's *The Best American Poetry*. Her third book for children, *Yellow Elephant,* was recently named a *Boston Globe*/Horn Book Honor Book. She teaches in Vermont College's M.F.A. in Writing Program.

QUINN LATIMER is a poet and editor based in New York City, where she works for *Modern Painters*. Her poems have appeared in *The Paris Review, Boston Review, Seneca Review, Phoebe,* and elsewhere. In collaboration with Paolo Thorsen-Nagel, she is currently translating the poems of Hans Arp.

BRIAN LEARY is the founding editor of the online journal, *42opus*. Other poems are forthcoming in *New Orleans Review* and *Third Coast*.

STEPHANIE LENOX lives in Tempe, Arizona and is coeditor of the online literary journal *Blood Orange Review* (www.bloodorangereview.com). Her work is forthcoming in *Swink, DIAGRAM,* and *Gulf Coast,* among others. Her poem "Making Love to the Leopard Man" is part of a series inspired by the *Guinness Book of World Records*.

"Pilgrimage" is KAREN LEPRI's first published poem. Her historical writing appears in *Yards and Gates: Gender in Harvard and Radcliffe History* (Palgrave, 2004). She holds degrees from Harvard Univserity and University of Massachusetts Boston. She was a teacher for five years in Boston and New York and now lives on Cape Cod where she is writing and applying to M.F.A. programs.

MICHAEL MCGRIFF was born and raised in Coos Bay, Oregon. A former Michener Fellow at the University of Texas at Austin, he is currently a Stegner Fellow at Stanford University. He received the 2005 Ruth Lilly Fellowship from *Poetry* magazine, and his poems have appeared in *Poetry, Northwest Review, Hayden's Ferry Review, Mid-American Review,* and elsewhere.

CHRISTINIA MENGERT holds an M.F.A. in Literary Arts from Brown University and is currently pursuing a Ph.D. in English/creative writing at the University of Denver. Her poems have appeared in *Salt, American Letters and Commentary, Aufgabe, Phoebe, Typo,* and *Versal,* among other journals. Her first manuscript, *The Last Night of Polaris,* was recently a finalist for the National Poetry Series and Nightboat Poetry Award.

DARREN MORRIS's poems have appeared in *American Poetry Review, RATTLE, Bitter Oleander, River Styx, Diner,* and others. His short story "Paper Airplane Engineer" recently won second prize in *Style Weekly*'s Annual Fiction Contest, and his fiction also earned him a fellowship from Virginia Commission of the Arts. He recieved his M.F.A. from Virginia Commonwealth University in 1998.

JAY NEBEL recently drove a U-Haul truck from Eugene, Oregon to Flagstaff, Arizona, where he now lives with his wife and two chihuahuas. He would like to dedicate his poem "The Romantic" to his only sister, Suzy, for all of her bravery.

JILL OSIER's work appears in *Black Warrior Review, The Gettysburg Review, The Literary Review, Poetry, Prairie Schooner,* and *32 Poems*. She's been living in Alaska and Iowa.

PHILIP PARDI has poems in recent issues of *Gettysburg Review, Seneca Review,* and *Mid-American Review*. He teaches at Bard College.

KIKI PETROSINO is a recent graduate of the Iowa Writers' Workshop. Her work has appeared, or is forthcoming, in *42opus; Contrary; Forklift, Ohio;* and *POOL*. She lives in Iowa City.

ALISON POWELL's poetry has previously appeared, or is forthcoming, in journals such as *Black Warrior Review, AGNI, Puerto del Sol, Meridian,* and *Poet Lore*. She currently resides in San Francisco, California, where she works for a nonprofit organization advocating for criminal justice and prison reform.

GRETCHEN PRIMACK's recent credits include *The Paris Review, Prairie Schooner, FIELD, New Orleans Review, Tampa Review, Rhino,* and others, and her manuscript *Fiery Cake* has been shortlisted for several prizes. She lives in the Hudson Valley with many beloved animals and a beloved human.

STEPHANIE ROGERS attended The Ohio State University and the University of Cincinnati. She is a two-time nominee for the Ruth Lilly Poetry Fellowship, and her work has appeared, or is forthcoming in *Cream City Review, Madison Review, Roanoke Review, Spoon River Poetry Review,* and *The Pinch.* She is currently pursuing an M.F.A. in poetry at the University of North Carolina, Greensboro.

NATALIE SHAPERO's poetry has appeared in *32 Poems, Southwest Review, River Styx,* and elsewhere. She lives in Columbus, Ohio.

MEG SHEVENOCK recently graduated from the University of Florida's M.F.A. program in poetry. She's been published in *32 Poems, Passages North,* and *Puerto del Sol,* and has been a finalist in the *Atlantic Monthly's* 2006 student writing competition. This fall she will pursue an M.F.A. in sculpture at The Ohio State University.

BARBARA BUCKMAN STRASKO is a Literacy Consultant for the School District of Lancaster. Her poems have appeared in *Rhino, Margie: The American Journal of Poetry, Ellipsis, Poet Lore* and others. She earned her M.F.A. in Creative Writing from Vermont College.

AUTUMN WATTS is an M.F.A. graduate of Cornell, where she now teaches, most recently at the Doha, Qatar campus. Her poetry and fiction have appeared in *AGNI, Indiana Review, Mode,* and *Portland Review.* She is currently working to complete her first novel.

JOE WILKINS was born and raised on a sheep ranch north of the Bull Mountains in eastern Montana, and he now teaches and writes in Moscow, Idaho. His poems, essays, and stories have appeared, or are forthcoming, in *The Georgia Review, Northwest Review, Swink, Boulevard,* and other literary journals. His first chapbook, *Ragged Point Road,* will be published by Main Street Rag Press this winter.

SUSAN SETTLEMYRE WILLIAMS's poetry has appeared in *River City, Shenandoah, storySouth, Barrow Street, Mississippi Review,* and other journals, and in *DIAGRAM.2.* She recently won the 2006 *Diner* Poetry Contest. Her book-length manuscript has been a finalist in several competitions, and her chapbook *Possession* is forthcoming from Finishing Line Press. She is book review editor and associate literary editor of *Blackbird*.

BARBARA YIEN grew up in the San Francisco Bay Area. Her poems have appeared in *42opus, Margie,* and elsewhere. She lives in Davis, California and works as a textbook editor.

VINCENT ZOMPA has traveled extensively, hitchhiking and eating at convenience stores along the way. He lives in Brooklyn and sometimes in Tokyo, where he vocalizes for *The Fallopian Disco Force*.

Acknowledgments

Andrew Allport's "An Unknown Shore" previously published in *ZYZZYVA*.

Teresa Ballard's "I Am Thinking Of My First Deer" previously published in
The Massachuetts Review.

Ciaran Berry's "Topography with Storm Petrels & Arctic Tern" previously published in
The Missouri Review.

Elizabeth Bradfield's "Cul-de-sac Linguistics" previously published in *Prairie Schooner*.

Jennifer Chapis's "The Beekeeper's Departure" previously published in *Florida Review* and
Backwards City Review.

Adam Chiles's "In Passing" previously published in *Poet Lore*.

Gary Joseph Cohen's "Bibliotalpidae" previously published in *Parthenon West Review*.

Eduardo C. Corral's "Se Me Olvidó Otra Vez" previously published in *Poetry Northwest*.

Gaynell Gavin's "Remembering the Bear" previously published in *Intersections*, a chapbook by
Main Street Rag Publishing.

Lisa Gluskin's "Spring Forward" previously published in *Michigan Quarterly Review*.

Jessica Goodfellow's "What You See If You Use Water as a Mirror" previously published in
Beloit Poetry Journal.

Theo Hummer's "Embalm" previously published in *Sentence*.

Anna Journey's "Lucifer's Panties at Lowe's Garden Center" previously published in *Gulf Coast*.

Andrew Kozma's "Elegy for the End of the World" previously published in *Blue Mesa Review*.

Julie Larios's "Double Abecedarian: Please Give Me" previously published in *The Georgia Review*
and *Best American Poetry 2006*.

Quinn Latimer's "Chekhov's Photograph" previously published in *Seneca Review*.

Brian Leary's "Self-Portrait as Suicide Girl's Skirt" previously published in
Washington Square Review.

Stephanie Lenox's "Making Love to Leopard Man" previously published in *Hayden's Ferry Review*.

Michael McGriff's "Iron" previously published in *Northwest Review*.

Christina Mengert's "Apology" previously published in *Phoebe*.

Jill Osier's "Bedful of Nebraskas" previously published in *Black Warrior Review*.

Philip Pardi's "Wintering" previously published in *Mid-American Review*.

Kiki Petrosino's "You Have Made a Career of Not Listening" previously published in *42opus*.

Gretchen Primack's "Colors" previously published in *FIELD*.
Stephanie Rogers's "Symphony for Red" previously published in *Spoon River Poetry Review*.
Natalie Shapero's "Nymphet" previously published in *32 Poems Magazine*.
Barbara Buckman Strasko's "Solo in the Snow" previously published in *Rhino*.
Autumn Watts's "Dry Lake, Nevada, 1983" previously published in *AGNI*.
Susan Settlemyre Williams's "Lighter" previously published in *Diner*.

Participating Writing Programs

American University
M.F.A. Program in Creative Writing
Department of Literature
4400 Massachusetts Avenue N.W.
Washington, DC 20036

Bowling Green State University
Creative Writing Program
Department of English
Bowling Green, OH 43403
www.bgsu.edu/departments/
    creative-writing/home.html

Brooklyn College
M.F.A. Program in Creative Writing
Department of English
2900 Bedford Avenue
Brooklyn, NY 11210

Brown University
Program in Literary Arts
Box 1923
Providence, RI 02912
www.brown.edu/Departments/Literary_Arts/

Columbia University Writing Division
School of the Arts
Dodge Hall
2960 Broadway, Room 400
New York, NY 10027-6902

Emerson College
M.F.A. in Creative Writing
120 Boylston Street
Boston, MA 02116-1596

Fine Arts Work Center in Provincetown
Writing Fellowship
24 Pearl Street
Provincetown, MA 02657
www.fawc.org

Florida International University
M.F.A. Program in Creative Writing
Department of English, Biscayne Bay Camp
3000 N.E. 151st Street
North Miami, FL 33181

Florida State University
Department of English
Williams Building
Tallahassee, FL 32306-1580
english.fsu.edu/crw/index.html

Hollins University
Creative Writing Program
P.O. Box 9677
Roanoke, VA 24020

Johns Hopkins University
The Writing Seminars
135 Gilman Hall
3400 North Charles Street
Baltimore, MD 21218-2690

Kansas State University
Creative Writing Program
Department of English
108 ECS Building
Manhattan, KS 66506
www.ksu.edu/english/programs/cw.html

Louisiana State University
English Department
260 Allen
Baton Rouge, LA 70803
english.lsu.edu/dept/programs/
    creative_writing

McNeese State University
Program in Creative Writing
P.O. Box 92655
Lake Charles, LA 70609
www.mfa.mcneese.edu/

Minnesota State University, Mankato
Creative Writing Program
230 Armstrong Hall
Mankato, MN 56001
www.english.mnsu.edu

San Francisco State University
Creative Writing Department
College of Humanities
1600 Holloway Avenue
San Francisco, CA 94132-4162

Sewanee Writers' Conference
735 University Avenue
Sewanee, TN 37383-1000
www.sewaneewriters.org

Texas A&M University
Creative Writing Program
Deptartment of English
Blocker 227 – TAMU 4227
College Station, TX 77843-4227

Texas State University
M.F.A. Program in Creative Writing
Department of English
601 University Drive, Flowers Hall
San Marcos, TX 78666
www.txstate.edu

Texas Tech University
Creative Writing Program
English Department
TTU
Lubbock, TX 79409-3091
www.english.ttu.edu/cw/

The Asian American Writers' Workshop
16 West 32nd Street Suite 10A
New York, NY 10001
www.aaww.org

The Bread Loaf Writers' Conference
Middlebury College
Kirk Alumni Center
Middlebury, VT 05753
www.middlebury.edu

The New School
Graduate Writing Program
66 West 12th Street, Room 505
New York, NY 10001

University of Alabama
Program in Creative Writing
Department of English
P.O. Box 870244
Tuscaloosa, AL 35487-0244
www.bama.ua.edu/~writing

University of Alaska
Fairbanks Program in Creative Writing
Department of English
P.O. Box 755720
Fairbanks, AK 99775-5720
www.uaf.edu/english/

University of Arizona
Creative Writing Program
Department of English
Modern Languages Bldg. #67
Tucson, AZ 85721-0067

University of Arkansas
Program in Creative Writing
Department of English
333 Kimpel Hall
Fayetteville, AR 72701
www.uark.edu/depts/english/PCWT.html

University of California, Davis
Graduate Creative Writing Program
Department of English
Davis, CA 95616

University of Central Florida
Graduate Program in Creative Writing
Department of English
P.O. Box 161346
Orlando, FL 32816-1346
www.english.ucf.edu

University of Colorado at Boulder
Creative Writing Program
Department of English
Campus Box 226
Boulder, CO 80309-0226

University of Denver
Creative Writing Program
Department of English
2140 South Race Street
Denver, CO 80208
www.du.edu/english/gradcwr.html

University of Florida
Creative Writing Program
Department of English
P.O. Box 11730
Gainesville, FL 32611-7310
www.english.ufl.edu/crw/

University of Houston
Creative Writing Program
Department of English
R. Cullen 229
Houston, TX 77204-3015

University of Idaho
Creative Writing Program
Department of English
Moscow, ID 83843-1102
www.class.uidaho.edu/english/CW/
    mfaprogram.html

University of Iowa
Program in Creative Writing
102 Dey House
507 North Clinton Street
Iowa City, IA 52242

University of Maryland
Creative Writing Program
Department of English
3119F Susquehanna Hall
College Park, MD 20742
www.english.umd.edu/programs/
    CreateWriting/index.html

University of Massachusetts
M.F.A. Program for Poets and Writers
Bartlett Hall
130 Hicks Way
Amherst, MA 01003-9269

University of Minnesota
M.F.A. Program in Creative Writing
Department of English
207 Church Street
SE Minneapolis, MN 55455
english.cla.umn.edu/creativewriting/
    program.html

University of Missouri-Columbia
Program in Creative Writing
Department of English
107 Tate Hall
Columbia, MO 65211
www.missouri.edu/~cwp

University of Missouri-St. Louis
M.F.A. in Creative Writing Program
Department of English
8001 Natural Bridge Road
St. Louis, MO 63121
www.umsl.edu~mfa

University of North Carolina, Greensboro
M.F.A. Writing Program
Dept. of English, 134 McIver Building
P.O. Box 26170
Greensboro, NC 27402-6170
www.uncg.edu/eng/mfa

University of Notre Dame
Creative Writing Program
356 O'Shaughnessy Hall
Notre Dame, IN 46556-0368
www.nd.edu/~alcwp/

University of Oregon
Program in Creative Writing
144 Columbia Hall
5243 University of Oregon
Eugene, OR 97403-5243
www.darkwing.uoregon.edu/~crwrweb/

University of San Francisco
Master of Arts in Writing Program
Program Office, Lone Mountain 340
2130 Fulton Street
San Francisco, CA 94117-1080

University of South Carolina
M.F.A. Program
Department of English
Columbia, SC 29208

University of Texas
Michener Center for Writers
J. Frank Dobie House
702 East Dean Keeton Street
Austin, TX 78705
www.utexas.edu/academic/mcw

University of Utah
Creative Writing Program
255 South Central Campus Drive
Room 3500
Salt Lake City, UT 84112

University of Virginia
Creative Writing Program
Department of English
P.O. Box 400121
Charlottesville, VA 22904-4121
www.engl.virginia.edu/cwp

University of Washington
Creative Writing Program
Box 354330
Seattle, WA 98195-4330

University of West Florida
Department of English
11000 University Parkway
Pensacola, FL 32514

University of Wisconsin-Madison
Wisconsin Institute for Creative Writing
Department of English
Helen C. White Hall
Madison, WI 53706
creativewriting.wisc.edu

University of Wisconsin-Madison
M.F.A. in Creative Writing
Department of English
600 N. Park St.
Madison, WI 53706

University of Wisconsin-Milwaukee
Creative Writing Program
Department of English Box 413
Milwaukee, WI 53201

University of Wyoming
Creative Writing Program
Department of English
P.O. Box 3353
Laramie, WY 82071-2000
www.uwyo.edu/creativewriting

Virginia Commonwealth University
M.F.A. in Creative Writing Program
Department of English
P.O. Box 842005
Richmond, VA 23284-2005

West Virginia University
Creative Writing Program
Department of English
P.O. Box 6269
Morgantown, WV 26506-6269
www.as.wvu.edu/english/

Western Michigan University
Graduate Program in Creative Writing
Department of English
Kalamazoo, MI 49008-5092

Canada

Sage Hill Writing Experience
Poetry Workshop, 2005
Box 1731
Saskatoon, SK S7K 3S1
www.sagehillwriting.ca

The Humber School for Writers
Correspondence Program in Creative Writing
205 Humber College Boulevard
Humber College
Toronto, ON M9W 5L7
www.humber.ca/creativeandperformingarts

University of British Columbia
Creative Writing Program
Buchanan E462-1866 Main Mall
Vancouver, BC V6T 1Z1
www.creativewriting.ubc.ca/

University of Calgary
Creative Writing Research Group (CWRG)
English Department
Creative Writing Program
Calgary, AB T2N 1N4
www.english.ucalgary.ca/creative/

Participating Magazines

32 Poems Magazine
English Department
TTU
Lubbock, TX 79409-3091
www.32poems.com

African American Review
Saint Louis University
Humanities 317
3800 Lindell Boulevard
St. Louis, MO 63108-3414
aar.slu.edu

AGNI
Boston University
Writing Program
236 Bay State Road
Boston, MA 02215

Alligator Juniper
Prescott College
220 Grove Avenue
Prescott, AZ 86301
www.prescott.edu/highlights/
    alligator_juniper/inex.html

American Poetry Review
117 South 17th Street
Suite 910
Philadelphia, PA 19103
www.aprweb.org

Arts & Letters
Georgia College & State University
Campus Box 89
Milledgeville, GA 31061
al.gcsu.edu

Bellevue Literary Review
NYU School of Medicine
Department of Medicine
550 First Avenue, OBV-A612
New York, NY 10016
www.BLReview.org

Bellingham Review
Western Washington University
MS-9053
Bellingham, WA 98225
www.wwu.edu/~bhreview

Beloit Poetry Journal
The Beloit Poetry Journal Foundation, Inc.
P.O. Box 151
Farmington, ME 04938
www.bpj.org

Black Warrior Review
University of Alabama
Box 862936
Tuscaloosa, AL 35486
www.webdelsol.com/bwr

Blackbird
Virginia Commonwealth University
Department of English
P.O. Box 843082
Richmond, VA 23284-3082
www.blackbird.vcu.edu

Blue Mesa Review
University of New Mexico
MSC03-2170, Humanities 274
Creative Writing Program
Albuquerque, NM 87131
www.unm.edu/~bluemesa

Calyx,
A Journal of Art and Literature by Women
Calyx, Inc.
P.O. Box B
Corvallis, OR 97339
www.calyxpress.org

Colorado Review
Colorado State University
The Center for Literary Publishing
Department of English
Fort Collins, CO 80523
coloradoreview.colostate.edu

CRAZYHORSE
College of Charleston
Department of English
66 George St.
Charleston, SC 29424
crazyhorse.cofc.edu

FIELD
Oberlin College Press
50 North Professor Street
Oberlin, OH 44074
www.oberlin.edu/ocpress

Gulf Coast
University of Houston
Department of English
Houston, TX 77204-3012

Gulf Stream Magazine
English Department
FIU Biscayne Bay Campus
3000 NE 151 Street
North Miami, FL 33181-3000

Harvard Review
Harvard University
Lamont Library
Cambridge, MA 02138
hcl.harvard.edu/harvardreview/

Hotel Amerika
Ohio University
English Dept. / 360 Ellis Hall
Athens, OH 45701
www.hotelamerika.net

IMAGE
3307 Third Avenue West
Seattle, WA 98119
www.imagejournal.org

Indiana Review
Indiana University
Ballantine Hall 465
1020 E. Kirkwood Ave.
Bloomington, IN 47405-7103
www.indiana.edu/~inreview

Michigan Quarterly Review
University of Michigan
3574 Rackham Bldg.
915 East Washington St.
Ann Arbor, MI 48019-1070
www.umich.edu/~mqr

Mid-American Review
Bowling Green State University
Department of English
Box W
Bowling Green, OH 43403

Mississippi Review
The University of Southern Mississippi
Box 5144
Hattiesburg, MS 39406-5144
www.mississippireview.com

New Letters
University of Missouri-Kansas City
5101 Rockhill Road
Kansas City, MO 64110
www.newletters.org

New Orleans Review
Loyola University
Box 195
New Orleans, LA 70118
www.loyno.edu/~noreview

Nimrod
The University of Tulsa
600 South College
Tulsa, OK 74104-3189
www.utulsa.edu/nimrod

Ninth Letter
234 English, Univ. of Illinois
608 S. Wright St.
Urbana, IL 61801
www.ninthletter.com

No Tell Motel
c/o Reb Livingston
11436 Fairway Drive
Reston, VA 20190
www.notellmotel.org

Northwest Review
University of Oregon
369 PLC New Line
Eugene, OR 97403

Pleiades
Central Missouri State University
Department of English and Philosophy
Warrensburg, MO 64093
www.cmsu.edu/englphil/pleiades

Poetry International
San Diego State University
Department of English & Comparative
Literature
5500 Campanile
San Diego, CA 92182-8140

Prairie Schooner
University of Nebraska-Lincoln
201 Andrews Hall
P.O. Box 880334
Lincoln, NE 68501-9988
prairieschooner.unl.edu

Salamander
Attn: Jennifer Barber
Suffolk University English Department
41 Temple Street
Boston, MA 02114
www.salamandermag.org

Seneca Review
Hobart and William Smith Colleges
Pulteney Street
Geneva, NY 14456
www.hws.edu/SenecaReview

Sentence
Firewheel Editions
Box 7
181 White St.
Danbury, CT 06810
www.firewheel-editions.org

Stirring: A Literary Collection
501 S. Elm St #1
Champaign, IL 61820
www.sundress.net/stirring/

The Antioch Review
Antioch University
P.O. Box 148
Yellow Springs, OH 45387
www.review.antioch.edu

The Cream City Review
University of Milwaukee-Wisconsin
Department of English
P.O. Box 413
Milwaukee, WI 53201
www.uwm.edu/Dept/English/ccr/

The Eleventh Muse
Poetry West
P.O. Box 2413
Colorado Springs, CO 80901
www.poetrywest.org/muse.htm

The Georgia Review
The University of Georgia
Athens, GA 30602-9009
www.uga.edu/garev

The Gettysburg Review
Gettysburg College
Gettysburg, PA 17325-1491
www.gettysburgreview.com

The Greensboro Review
University of North Carolina, Greensboro
English Department
134 McIver, P.O. Box 26170
Greensboro, NC 27402-6170
www.greenshororeview.com

The Hudson Review
684 Park Avenue
New York, NY 10021
www.hudsonreview.com

The Kenyon Review
Kenyon College
Walton House
Gambier, OH 43022-9623
www.kenyonreview.org

The Los Angeles Review
Red Hen Press
P.O. Box 3537
Granada Hills, CA 91394

The Massachusetts Review
University of Massachusetts
South College
Amherst, MA 01003
www.massreview.org

The Missouri Review
University of Missouri
1507 Hillcrest Hall
Columbia, MO 65211

The National Poetry Review
P.O. Box 4041
Felton, CA 95018
www.nationalpoetryreview.com

The New Hampshire Review
P.O. Box 322
Nashua, NH 03061-0322
www.newhampshirereview.com

The Powhatan Review
4936 Farrington Drive
Virginia Beach, VA 23455
www.powhatanreview.com

The Southwest Review
Southern Methodist University
307 Fondren Library West
P.O. Box 750374
Dallas, TX 75275-0374
www.southwestreview.org

The Texas Review
Sam Houston State Univeristy
P.O. Box 2146
Huntsville, TX 77341-2146

The Tusculum Review
Tusculum College
Department of English
60 Shiloh Road
Greenville, TN 37743

The William & Mary Review
William & Mary
P.O. Box 8795
Williamsburg, VA 23187-8795

Third Coast
Western Michigan University
Department of English
Kalamazoo, MI 49008-5092

Three Candles Journal
P.O. Box 1817
Burnsville, MN 55337
www.threecandles.org

ZYZZYVA
P.O. Box 590069
San Francisco, CA 94159-0069
www.zyzzyva.org